Been There!
BRAZIL

Annabel Savery

W

FRANKLIN WATTS
LONDON • SYDNEY

Facts about Brazil

Population: 184 million

Capital city: Brasília

Currency: Real (R$)

Main language: Portuguese

Rivers: Amazon, São Francisco, Paraná, Tocantins

Area: 8,511,965 square kilometres (3,286, 488 square miles)

 An Appleseed Editions book

First published in 2011 by Franklin Watts
338 Euston Road, London NW1 3BH

Franklin Watts Australia
Hachette Children's Books
Level 17/207 Kent St, Sydney, NSW 2000

© 2011 Appleseed Editions

Created by Appleseed Editions Ltd,
Well House, Friars Hill, Guestling,
East Sussex TN35 4ET

Planning and production by Discovery Books Limited
www.discoverybooks.net
Designed by Ian Winton
Edited by Annabel Savery
Map artwork by Stefan Chabluk
Picture research by Tom Humphrey

ISBN 978 1 4451 0352 5

Dewey Classification: 981'.065

A CIP catalogue for this book is available from the British Library.

Picture Credits: Alamy Images: p11 (Holger Mette), p17 (imagebroker); Arthur Mota: p16; Corbis: p8 (Antonio Lacerda/EFE), p9 (Mike
Theiss/National Geographic), p14 (Atlantide Phototravel), p15 (Jeremy Horner), p25 bottom (Wolfgang Kaehler), p26 (Sergio Moraes/
Reuters); Discovery Picture Library: p18 (Ed Parker); Getty Images: pp6-7 (Steve Allen), p13 bottom (SambaPhoto/Cassio
Vasconcellos), p19 (Luis Veiga), p20 (Rolf Richardson), p24 (AFP), p29 (Nico Tondini); Istockphoto: p12 & p31 (Agenturfotograf),
p21 top (luoman), p22 bottom (thejack); Nature Picture Library: p21 bottom (Mark Carwardine); Shutterstock: p2 (tristian
quesnelle), p5 top (Dr Morley Read), p5 middle (gary yim), p10 (jbor), p13 top (Peter Leahy), p22 top (guentermanaus), p23
(guentermanaus), p25 top (ecoventurestravel), p27 (guentermanaus), p28 top (ostill); Wikimedia: p28 bottom (Cayambe).

Cover photos: Shutterstock: main (Elder Vieira Salles), left (ostill), right (Vinicius Tupinamba).

Franklin Watts is a division of Hachette Children's Books, an Hachette UK company.
www.hachette.co.uk

Contents

Off to Brazil!

We are going on holiday to Brazil.

Brazil is an enormous country in the continent of South America. There are high mountains and flat areas called plains.

There are also huge rainforests. We are going to many different places so there will be lots of travelling. I can't wait to go there!

Here are some things I know about Brazil...

- Brazil is the largest country in South America and the fifth largest in the world.

- The River Amazon is in Brazil. It is 6,480 kilometres (4,026 miles) long. It is one of the longest rivers in the world.

- There are lots of festivals in Brazil. These are big celebrations with music and dancing.

On our trip I'm going to find out lots more!

Arriving in Rio de Janeiro

From home we fly to Rio de Janeiro. This is a city on the eastern coast of Brazil. When we arrive, it is hot and sticky. We take a bus from the airport to the city centre.

We leave our luggage at the hotel and set out to explore. First we take the **cog railway** to the **summit** of a peak called Corcovado.

On the summit of Corcovado is a huge statue of Christ the Redeemer. At 38 metres (124 feet) high it towers above us.

From up here there is a great view. Mum and Dad take lots of pictures. We can see the tall buildings of the city. Beyond the buildings the sea is very blue and there are jagged green hills everywhere we look.

Carnival time!

Wherever we go in Rio, people tell us about Carnival.

Carnival is a big celebration that is held every year. It lasts for four days and three nights. There are parades, shows, music and dancing. Carnival celebrates the time before **Lent** begins.

There are other festivals in Brazil too. Some are religious celebrations, others mark important days in the country's history, such as Independence Day.

Lots of people in Brazil are Roman Catholics. This religion was brought to Brazil by Portuguese explorers.

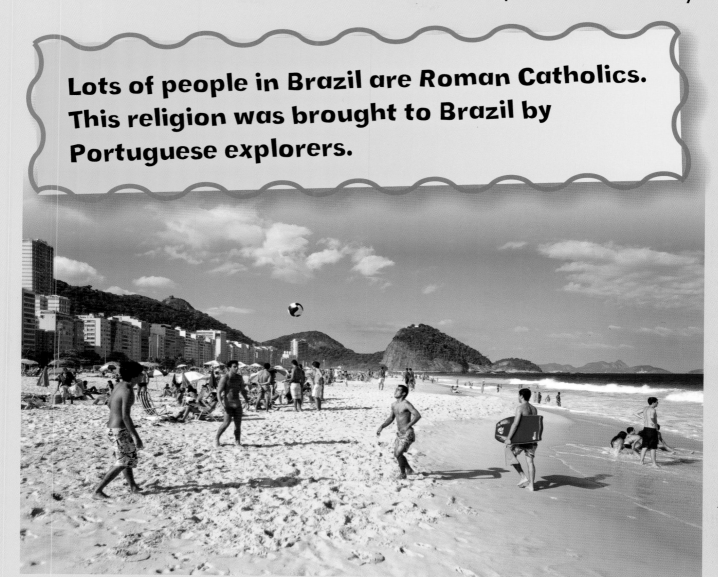

Before we leave we go to the beautiful Copacabana beach. There are lots of people here. Some are tourists on holiday, like us. Others are people who live in Rio and like to come here at the weekend. They are playing football and beach volleyball.

Out and about in São Paulo

The next place we are going to visit is São Paulo city. It is the biggest city in Brazil. As we arrive, we can see tall skyscrapers.

There are lots of offices, and Dad explains that many businesses are based here.

The city is crowded. People from all over the world live in São Paulo. Many Europeans and Japanese people have come to live in the city.

The streets are busy. Some people are dressed for work; others are shopping.

People are selling food from stalls; some of them are children.

Children have to go to school from the age of seven to 14. However, some families are poor and their children miss school to work and to help earn money.

The Iguaçu falls

From São Paulo we fly to the town of Foz de Iguaçu. The Iguaçu Falls are nearby. They are on the border between Argentina and Brazil.

The Iguaçu Falls are amazing. The noise of rushing water is very loud.

The falls are made when the River Iguaçu falls over a sheer drop. At the top of the falls the river is four kilometres (2.5 miles) wide. When it falls it splits into 275 waterfalls!

The falls are in a national park. Many types of wildlife live here. Butterflies flutter about. Toucans, monkeys, lizards and deer live here too.

Further north from the falls on the River Paraná is the 8-km (5-mile) wide Itaipu dam. The dam creates hydroelectric power. It provides electricity for Brazil and Paraguay.

Sights in Salvador

From the Iguaçu Falls we fly to Salvador. It is a busy, bustling city.

Salvador is on the coast and is an important port. Brazil **exports** many products from here, such as tropical fruit, cocoa and soya beans.

Women called *Bahianas* are selling food from big trays. They are dressed in traditional clothes.

We try *acarajé*. It is made from black-eyed peas that are rolled into a ball and deep-fried. Then this is split open and stuffed with spicy shrimp paste. Yum!

Lots of the food in Salvador has African origins. When the Portuguese first came to settle in Brazil they brought over African slaves to work on sugar plantations. African culture and traditions have been passed down to people who live in Brazil today.

Exploring Recife

Our next stop is the city of Recife. I like exploring Recife, but it is easy to get lost. The streets are narrow and winding. There are high, modern buildings, old-looking churches, and busy markets.

One of the markets is called the *Mercado São José*. Inside the stalls sell fish, meat and vegetables. Others sell handicrafts. Mum buys me a necklace made from seeds.

On the outskirts of the city the buildings are different. They are not tall and smart like in the city centre. Most are simple and small. These areas are called *favelas* or shanty-towns. People with little money live here. There are *favelas* in most Brazilian cities.

On the bus

Next we are going to travel to Belem. This is a city at the mouth of the River Amazon. It is going to be a long journey.

From Recife we have to catch two buses to get to Belem. The whole journey will take 36 hours!

Sugar cane

On the way we travel through sugar plantations. Farming is important in Brazil. Mum says many crops are grown to feed the country's people and also to export.

One fifth of Brazil's population work in agriculture. Most live in small villages in **rural** areas. They grow crops and raise livestock.

Coffee beans

One of the main crops is coffee. Brazil produces about a quarter of the world's coffee. It is grown in southern areas near São Paulo.

The River Amazon

It is very hot and **humid** when we get to Belem. We are now very near the **equator**.

Belem is the port city of the Amazon. Boats come and go from here taking people and **merchandise** up-river. We are going to take a boat from here up the river to the city of Manaus.

We have a cabin on the boat. The journey is going to take five days. Mum has filled a basket with food for the trip, but there are meals served on board too.

The River Amazon is enormous. The area surrounding it is called Amazonia. This is made up of dense tropical rainforest and covers more than half of Brazil.

On the boat I look out for an Amazon River dolphin. In Brazil they are called *boutu vermelho*, which means 'red dolphin'.

The city of Manaus

I feel a bit wobbly when we get off the boat in Manaus. Mum says it's because we've been moving for a long time.

Manaus is the capital of the state of Amazonas. There are high, modern buildings and traditional wooden houses. I am surprised to see such a big city in the rainforest.

At lunchtime we go to a restaurant. Fish is a popular food here and we all choose fish dishes. I have *caldeirada*. This is a fish and vegetable soup that originally came from Portugal.

In the evening we go to the *Teatro Amazonas*. It is a huge building with a coloured dome on the top and archways at the entrance. Inside it is decorated with patterns in bright colours.

In the rainforest

For a few days we are going to explore the rainforest around Manaus. Our guide is called Elso.

River Negro

River Solimões

First, Elso takes us to the place where two rivers meet, the Solimões and the Negro. The two rivers are different colours. The Solimões is yellow-brown and the River Negro is blue-black. Where they meet the two colours mix together.

Elso explains about the animals that live in the rainforest. They all sound strange to me. Fish called piranhas live in the river, as well as dolphins, alligators and **caimans.**

Caiman

Elso tells us about *caboclos* or 'the people of the forest'. They live in settlements near the river and have little contact with people who live in the cities. The *caboclos* know the forest very well and live on what they can find there.

Leaving the rainforest

As we leave we fly over more of the rainforest. It is a huge area. Dad says that there are some parts that have only been seen by people who live in the forest. They are no maps of these areas.

People explore the rainforest for different reasons. Some go to find out about plants. Others go to find out about people who live in the rainforest. Some scientists are even looking for new medicines in the rainforest.

There are **indigenous** Indian tribes who live deep in the rainforest. Some have no contact with the outside world.

There are areas where the trees have been cut down. Wood from the trees in the rainforest can be very valuable. People also clear land for buildings and growing crops. This harms the forest and the animals and people that live there.

The capital city

Our flight lands in Brasília, the capital city of Brazil. The government is based here. This is our last stop in Brazil.

In the afternoon we go to see the cathedral. It is made of lots of spikes in a circle. Inside, the beautiful roof is made of coloured glass.

A new city

Rio de Janeiro used to be the capital of Brazil. The government built the city of Brasília to encourage people to move inland. On 1 April 1960 the new city was opened and people moved in.

In the evening we go to a restaurant for our last meal before we fly home. I have *feijoada*. This is the national dish. It is made from black beans, pork, potatoes and herbs and spices. Feijoada is served with slices of orange. It is very tasty.

My first words in Portuguese

Many languages are spoken in Brazil. The most common and official language is Portuguese. There are words from other languages mixed in too.

Bom dia (*say* **Boom dee ah**)	Hello
Até logo (*say* **At-ay la-goh**)	Goodbye
Como vai? (*say* **Como vaai**)	How are you?
Como é seu nome? (*say* **Como ehy seo nameh**)	What is your name?
Meu nome é Antony. (*say* **Meo namay ehy Anthony**)	My name is Anthony.

Counting 1-10

1 **um/uma**   2 **dois/duas**   3 **três**
4 **quatro**   5 **cinco**   6 **seis**   7 **sete**
8 **oito**   9 **nove**   10 **dez**

Words to remember

caiman a reptile in the crocodile family

cog railway a type of railway that can travel up steep hills and slopes

equator an imaginary great circle around the Earth's surface. It is equal in distance from the north and south poles.

export to sell goods to another country

humid damp, moist air

hydroelectric able to produce electricity using moving water

indigenous people who originally come from a place

Lent the 40 days before Easter

merchandise products that are bought and sold in businesses

plantation an area where large amounts of a crop are grown in huge fields

rural in or near the countryside

summit the top of a hill or mountain

Index

Learning more about Brazil

Books

Brazil (Countries of the World) Brian Dicks, Evans Brothers Ltd, 2005.
Brazil (Discover Countries) Ed Parker, Wayland, 2009.
Brazil (World in Focus) Simon Scoones, Wayland, 2008.
Rainforest (Eye Wonder) Dorling Kindersley, 2004.

Websites

National Geographic Kids, People and places
   http://kids.nationalgeographic.com/places/find/brazil
Geography for kids, Geography online and Geography games
   http://www.kidsgeo.com/index.php
SuperKids Geography directory, lots of sites to help with geography learning.
   http://www.super-kids.com/geography.html

1970s

Sally Hewitt

W

FRANKLIN WATTS
LONDON•SYDNEY

I can remember the 1970s

First published in 2003 by Franklin Watts
96 Leonard Street, London EC2A 4XD

Franklin Watts Australia
45-51 Huntley Street
Alexandria, NSW 2015

© Franklin Watts 2003

Series editor: Sarah Peutrill
Series design: White Design
Art director: Jonathan Hair
Picture researcher: Diana Morris

A CIP catalogue record
for this book is available from
the British Library

ISBN 0 7496 4868 6

Printed in Malaysia

Picture credits:
AP/Topham: 4. Bettmann/Corbis: 11. Central Press/Hulton
Archive: 17. Mary Evans PL: 10t, 13. Lynn Goldsmith/Corbis: 23t.
Henry Grant/Mary Evans PL: 16. Sally Greenhill/Sally & Richard
Greenhill: 6b. Hulton-Deutsch Collection/Corbis: 20b. Colin
Jones/Topham: 7. Keystone/Hulton Archive: 14-15b, 29t. Kobal
Collection: front cover drop-in. Lucas Films/Kobal Collection:
24. Graham Morris/Evening Standard/Hulton Archive: front cover b. Popperfoto: 27,
28b, 29b. Neal Preston/Corbis: front cover tl, 21. J. Pridmore/Popperfoto: 19. Science
Museum, London/HIP: 12. Topham Picturepoint: 8, 9, 23b, 25, 26b. TRH Pictures: front
cover cr. UPPA.co.uk: 22b. Michael Webb/Keystone/Hulton Archive: 20t.

Whilst every attempt has been made to clear copyright should there be any inadvertent
omission please apply in the first instance to the publisher regarding rectification.

The author and publisher would like to thank everyone who contributed
their memories and personal photographs to this book.

Contents

Introduction

A TURBULENT TIME

In 1970 the voting age was lowered from 21 to 18, giving young people a say in politics for the first time. The 1970s, the first decade in which they could use their new power, was a time of political turbulence. In 1973, the price of oil rose bringing with it the threat of petrol shortages and causing the cost of living to go up all over the world. Britain suffered from inflation – a drop in the value of money.

⬆ Miners' wives march in support of their husbands' claim for more pay.

STRIKES

In Britain, a series of strikes began that were to cause disruption and chaos. In 1973, a miners' strike led to a shortage of coal supplies to power stations. To save energy, the government introduced a three-day week. More strikes followed leading to the 'Winter of Discontent' in 1979 with rubbish left rotting in the streets and hospitals turning patients away.

LIFE STYLES

But the 1970s were not all bad. In general, people were able to enjoy more leisure time. Cheap package holidays meant that more people could afford to go abroad on holiday. Fast-food restaurants and new, imported ingredients changed the way that people ate. Colour televisions gradually replaced black-and-white televisions in the home.

MUSIC AND FASHION

Music and fashion defied the atmosphere of gloom. In the early 1970s, glam rock bands grew their hair, painted their faces and wore brightly-coloured, sparkling clothes. At the end of the decade, punk rock bands spiked their hair and wore studs and black leather in protest against the politicians.

BLOCKBUSTERS

Hugely successful films called blockbusters packed the cinemas with movie-goers. *Jaws*, the story of a man-eating shark, made a generation nervous of going into the water. Toys, stickers and posters based on the movie *Star Wars* filled the shops.

THEY CAN REMEMBER

In this book six people share their memories of what it was like to live in Britain in the 1970s. They each have a story to tell in their own section, but they also add other memories throughout the book.

Carole Creegen

Carole lived in west London with her husband and children during the 1970s. She remembers what community life was like.

Sue Anderson

Sue describes growing up in the 1970s as the daughter of Jamaican immigrants. The IRA bombing campaign in London affected her in a very direct way.

David Bedford

David grew up in Devon, and recalls some of his many childhood adventures.

Andrew King

Andrew lived in Bromley and was a fan of 1970s' music, especially glam and punk rock.

Nifa Vaz

Nifa came to Britain as a Ugandan refugee when she was nine years old.

Helen Passey

Helen was at school and university during the 1970s. She remembers the strikes and the Winter of Discontent.

Carole Creegen's story

Carole, 1971

GOOD NEIGHBOURS

Carole and her husband Peter lived in a friendly community in west London. They had four children, Lucy, Maria and the twins, Tom and Emma. The children played outside in the street. Carole didn't worry about them. Neighbours always kept an eye on each others' children and made sure they were safe.

NEIGHBOURHOOD ASSOCIATION

Carole helped to set up a neighbourhood association in the 1970s that is still very active today. It involved shopping for those who couldn't get out, and driving people to hospital.

↓ Local police officers were well-known.

> *An elderly widow who lived two or three doors away had always dined out with her husband so she had never cooked a meal in her life. I took her a cooked meal at least once a week. She used to say, 'I don't know why you do this for me. I wouldn't do it for you!'*

LOCAL BOBBY

The local police officer was a familiar figure to Carole, riding around the streets on his bicycle. Everyone knew him by name. He was the first person they turned to if there was any trouble or if help was needed.

> *Our local bobby would be there every day. What he didn't know about our neighbourhood wasn't worth knowing! He would always stop and chat to the children.*

THE SILVER JUBILEE

In 1977, Queen Elizabeth II had been on the throne for 25 years. All over Britain bonfires were lit and street parties were held to celebrate her Silver Jubilee.

On Carole's street they decided to use the Silver Jubilee as a good excuse to get everyone together for a party. They asked the local police officer to help them get permission to close the road. When the day came, he joined the party too.

> 66 *We put up bunting [flags threaded onto string] and friends and family were all invited. In the afternoon we had games and fancy dress for the children followed by a traditional tea party with sandwiches, jelly, cakes and ice cream. In the evening we had an adult party with dancing to a steel band. Then the next morning, we had breakfast in the street as well.* 99

> ! **David remembers...**
> "*I took unusually big newspapers into school with pictures of the Jubilee. We cut them out and made a scrapbook. We had photocopied sheets of the Crown Jewels which we cut out and coloured in.*"

⬇ A Silver Jubilee street party in Belfast, 1977.

Life style

MONEY TO SPEND

In general people had more money to spend than ever before. They spent more on their homes: painting their walls brown and orange, and installing baths in colours named after the new exotic foods you could buy in the shops, such as avocado and aubergine. They were also able to spend more money on going out and could have holidays abroad.

⬆ Dark woods and the colour orange were popular in the 1970s.

NEW FOODS

Dinner parties became fashionable. People experimented with recipes from all over the world and tried out some of the new ingredients that became available in the shops – including garlic. Carole enjoyed experimenting with food.

> " I worked my way through a cookery book and cooked something new every day. We had lots of garlic and curries to get the children used to interesting food. We invited people for dinner and sat around in the kitchen talking into the small hours. "

❗ Andrew remembers...

"Our French teacher told us how to bite a clove of garlic and then swallow it quickly. That way, you didn't taste it but everyone else could smell it. The next day one of the boys bought along this bulb of garlic. We all tried it and the garlic did its magic. Two teachers that afternoon refused to teach us because of the smell!"

Babysitting

Carole remembers using the local babysitting rota so she could go out in the evening to the theatre and cinema with her husband.

> " *You had five points and lost one every time you went out. If you were out after midnight, you lost another point and another if you were out after 2 a.m. You gained a point when you babysat for someone else.* "

Holidays

• •

During the 1970s, package holidays offered cheap flights and accommodation in sunny places. Families who had always taken their holidays in Britain could now afford to go abroad. People set off for Spain's sandy beaches in their thousands, and also went on more adventurous holidays. Andrew and his family went to France in 1973.

"We stopped in a little French village for lunch but nothing was open except for this café that only had offal and tripe on the menu. Of course my brother and I wouldn't touch it. The old locals in the bar found the fact that we struggled with the food very amusing – which eventually, to our embarrassment, caused our father to stand up and sing the National Anthem at them in some sort of patriotic defiance!"

Fast-food restaurants

Fast-food restaurants, such as Wimpey and McDonald's began to be opened all over the country. Andrew remembers the public's reaction.

> " *When McDonald's hit Bromley in the 1970s it was big news. It provoked a huge number of letters to the local newspaper about the downfall of society. My friends and I thought it was extremely exciting. We went to McDonald's when we went into Bromley on our own.* "

← McDonald's still looks much the same today as it did in the 1970s.

Childhood adventures

David (middle), his brother Paul and sister Julie, 1977

GROWING UP IN DEVON

David and his brother Paul and sister Julie grew up in Braunton, Devon. The children roamed freely beyond the estate where they lived. They caught trout in the local stream, searched for brown crabs in the muddy estuary and slowworms in the fields. They had a lot of adventures.

GANGS

The children on David's estate belonged to different gangs. David's best friend in his gang was Trina.

⬆ Fishing was a popular pastime for children living in the country in the 1970s.

David and Trina in fancy dress.

> ❝ Trina had a dog called Jenny – a black Labrador – who was born on the same day as Trina. Jenny protected us if we came across other gangs and there were things like stone-throwing. But really, it was just kids playing around. ❞

SKATEBOARDING

David's adventures often got him into trouble. One day he tried to recreate *Starsky and Hutch* – a popular American television series about two undercover police officers. Every episode featured high-speed car chases and daring stunts.

> *I was coming down the hill on my skateboard. My friends had parked their skateboards and I thought, wouldn't it be great – like Starsky and Hutch – to jump off my skateboard and land on another skateboard and zoom off down the hill. Of course, I woke up hours later on the settee. I'd been concussed for a couple of hours. We didn't have protective clothing or helmets.*

Skateboard stunts took a great deal of practice.

RAID

One day, when David and his gang were bored, they planned a raid on a sweet shop.

> *It was like a jewelled grotto full of sweets we'd never had before. One at a time, we went in. I can't believe the shopkeepers didn't notice because we filled up a rucksack with sweets and went home with it on the back of a bike.*

GETTING CAUGHT

When David got home there was a knock on his door.

> *A police officer came in with his big hat on. I was frightened because he was very tall. He took his hat off, put it on the table and sat down. What he said has always stuck with me. He said – you're in trouble now, but you'll get out of trouble if you tell the truth. So we took the sweets back.*

A LESSON LEARNED

David never forgot the lesson he learned that night.

> *I'm glad it happened because I never got involved in serious trouble later on when I might have done.*

Childhood

AN ACTIVE CHILDHOOD

Without computer games to play with, and with only three television channels to watch, children were more likely to play outdoors in the 1970s. Chopper bikes, skateboards, pogo sticks and Spacehoppers were the toys every child longed for.

GREEN SHIELD STAMPS

Many of the toys were expensive, but if you couldn't afford them, Green Shield stamps could come to the rescue. Stamps were given to shoppers, depending on the amount they bought. When enough had been collected they could be exchanged for household items such as toasters, garden furniture and toys. David wanted a skateboard.

"My mum explained that we didn't have the money for skateboards. But our next-door neighbour worked in a garage where he was able to accumulate Green Shield stamps in huge amounts. He bought my brother and sister and me skateboards for Christmas with them."

CHOPPER BIKES

Chopper bikes were popular with boys in the 1970s. David's gang used to ride them.

"All the boys had Chopper bikes. You could carry a passenger on the long saddle. They had a gear shift with a little knob like on a car. The knob nearly always came off leaving just a metal spike. If you stopped suddenly and skidded off the saddle you could do yourself an injury! They were great for doing wheelies. Some boys only ever rode their bike with the front wheel up in the air."

⬇ The Chopper bike had L-shaped seats and long handlebars.

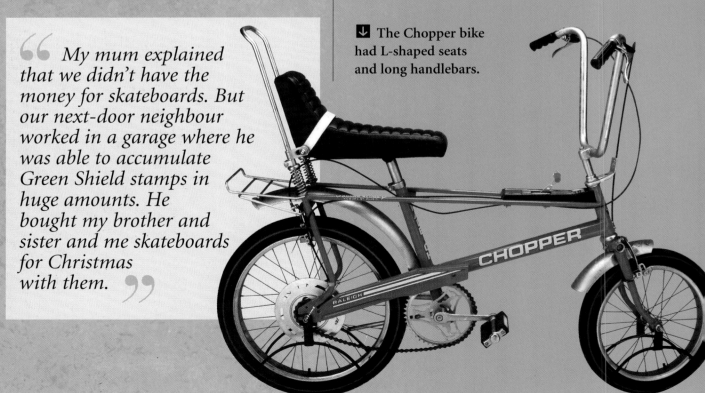

AFTER SCHOOL

Nifa moved to Britain from Uganda in 1972. Her new life was different in many ways from her childhood in Uganda. She started to enjoy so many different activities that there wasn't much time left for homework.

> " In Uganda, I got home from school, did my homework and read books. There wasn't much TV so I didn't get distracted by that.
>
> In England, I joined the choir, played netball, rounders and hockey – in fact I still play hockey now – I enjoyed all that. I watched TV. I used to watch Blue Peter and make all the things they showed. "

➡ Bouncing around on a Spacehopper.

! David remembers...

"We had Spacehoppers. I remember their rubbery smell. Ours had a little smiley face. We used to just bounce around the garden holding the ears."

POCKET MONEY

Pocket money was usually just enough to buy a few treats on a Saturday morning. Carole gave pocket money to her children.

> " The pocket money we gave our children was small compared with what children get now. It was a penny for every year of their life. But you could get quite a lot for a penny then. "

! Helen remembers...

"Our local church had a youth club that was run by the curate. It used to attract local kids. We used to play snooker and I remember playing chess. It was fun and a focus for meeting other kids who weren't at the same school as me. There wasn't a great deal else to do and certainly nothing that didn't cost money."

Escape to Britain

Nifa Vaz's story

Nifa, 1973

AMIN EXPELS ASIANS

In August 1972, Idi Amin, the military dictator of Uganda, a country in east Africa, announced that he planned to expel from the country all 50,000 Asians with British passports. Nifa was nine and living with her family in Uganda.

> *At the time, I didn't fully understand why we were being thrown out. I discovered much later that Amin asked the British government to loan him money. They said, 'We can't afford it and how are you going to pay it back?' So he decided to throw all the British Nationals out of the country.*

48 HOURS' NOTICE

Suddenly, in September, the Asians were given 48 hours to leave Uganda. 30,000 went to Britain and 20,000 went to Canada, the USA and India. Nearly everyone arrived with very little money and few possessions. Nifa's mother had all her money taken from her at Uganda Airport.

> *We did get our stuff out because we just had ordinary things like pots and pans. Other families had their crates ransacked for valuables. When they arrived in Britain, they opened the crates and found they were full of stones.*

MOVING TO LONDON

Camps were set up to receive the immigrants, but Nifa's family had a home to go to.

> *My mother's cousin lived in Ealing, west London. He said – if you don't want to go to a camp, you can have my flat. He very generously moved out and lived with a friend. We had to cook and do everything in one room.*

↗ Nifa's mother's Girl Guide Company being inspected by Idi Amin in 1972, just before Amin expelled the Asians.

GIRL GUIDES

Nifa's mother had been a Girl Guide Commissioner in Uganda. Lady Gibbs, a British Girl Guide Commissioner, gave the family help and support when they arrived in London.

> *The Girl Guides were very kind to us. Lady Gibbs took us to the theatre – to see* Treasure Island *which was wonderful because I had never seen live theatre.*

FINALLY SETTLED

After moving six times, the family finally settled down in Croydon and Nifa and her brother started going to school. Her mother worked as a supply teacher and her father found work in an office doing the accounts and book-keeping.

← An airlift was arranged to bring the Ugandan Asians to Stansted Airport in Britain.

Going to school

THE SCHOOL SYSTEM

At the beginning of the 1970s, most children went to one of three main kinds of state secondary school – grammar schools, technical schools and secondary modern schools.

GRAMMAR SCHOOL

To get into a grammar school, at the end of their primary schooling, pupils had to pass the Eleven Plus exam. If they failed it they would go to a technical school or secondary modern. Andrew passed his Eleven Plus.

⬇ A junior school classroom in the early 1970s.

> *I went to the local grammar school with some of my friends. I always felt it was a bit strange because a good friend of mine didn't get in. I thought this was ridiculous because as far as I was concerned he was as intelligent as everybody else.*
>
> *I remember my first day in 1972. We all sat in the drama studio and the headteacher came in wearing a large gown. He swept in – it was almost like Batman coming in. His sheer presence made everyone sit up straight. One boy was so overwhelmed he burst into tears and had to go home.*

COMPREHENSIVE SCHOOL

During the 1970s, comprehensive schools, introduced in the 1950s, at last largely replaced this system, and children no longer took the Eleven Plus or went to separate schools. Helen went to a comprehensive.

> *There were large numbers of pupils at my comprehensive school in Chester who weren't interested in education. Sometimes they would jump out of the windows during lessons.*

CALCULATORS

Calculators did not come into general use until the end of the 1970s, but Andrew remembers that there were other ways to do complicated calculations.

> *When I first went to secondary school, we used a slide rule to do calculations. We also had calculating machines with levers. By the end of the 1970s, scientific calculators with many functions were easily available.*

COMPUTERS

In the 1970s computers were only just coming into general use. Andrew remembers the first computer he ever used.

> *There was only one computer in the whole of Bromley – in the town hall. We used to write out instructions for it on punch cards.*

➡ A punch-card computer.

Different cultures

Sue, 1974

GROWING UP IN WANDSWORTH

Sue's parents left Jamaica for a new life in Britain in the 1950s with their four children. Sue and her younger sister were born in London. When they were teenagers growing up in Wandsworth they were influenced by both Caribbean and British culture.

> *My dad said, 'While we are in England, act like the English people.' But my culture is Jamaican and I made it that way. Even though there were more black and Asian girls than English girls at my school, I had to learn about everyone else's culture and history. I had to search for information about my own. Now my children know just as much about black culture as they do about white culture.*

! Nifa remembers...

"We started to get abuse in the area we were living in. There was one particular family who were openly not happy about us. They blocked the streets with their bicycles and wouldn't let us park. My mother said, 'I go to work and I pay my taxes. I'm going to call the police!' From then on, we weren't harassed."

DOMINOES

Sue's dad played a Caribbean version of dominoes.

> *You slam the dominoes down. My mum's light bulbs used to shake when my dad and his friends were playing upstairs.*

➡ Sue (far right in both photos) and family, in the 1970s.

Revellers at the Notting Hill Carnival in 1979.

DISCIPLINE

Sue's father was a disciplinarian.

> *Dad was strict on us girls going out. At midnight, if we weren't back, he would lock the door. We had to go round to where my mum was working nights and she'd come home and shout at him to let us in. He didn't allow us to have boys around.*

CARNIVAL

Sue started to go to the Notting Hill Carnival in the 1970s.

> *All the people who lived there used to sit outside and invite people in. They don't do it now. I followed the floats and danced the calypso. It was like a party on the street.*

CARIBBEAN FOOD

Sue was brought up on Caribbean food, including fish, rice, beans, yams, plantain and coconut.

> *We never used to have English food when we were growing up – except fish and chips on a Friday. We always had proper Caribbean food. If Mum was working Dad would prepare it.*

Sue now cooks Caribbean food for her family.

Fashion

'THE DECADE THAT TASTE FORGOT'
Fashion in the 1970s was anything but subtle. It was called 'the decade that taste forgot'. Bright colours and stripes were in. Girls wore tiny miniskirts and even smaller shorts called hot pants. Everyone wore flares and sleeveless sweaters called tank tops. The more hair you had, the better.

Sue loved wearing the latest fashions.

> 66 *I had brown and cream tops with matching flares and a striped tank top. We had winged-collared shirts with big cuffs and platform shoes.* 99

⬆ Flared trousers and big Afro hair became popular.

Sue had fishnet tights, made with an open-meshed material.

➡ Platform shoes were popular in the 1970s, with both men and women.

> 66 *I remember our budgie was flying around the room and he swooped down and got caught in my fishnet tights! He was pecking my leg and I was freaking out. My brothers were laughing.* 99

HAIR

In the 1970s, having the right hairstyle was just as important as wearing the right clothes. Sue had Afro hair.

> You could hide all kinds of things in your hair! I hid money in my Afro. One day I was combing my hair on the street without thinking anything about it. This police officer came up to me and said, 'That's a dangerous weapon.' I said, 'It's not, it's my Afro comb!' But after that, I bought one that you could fold like a fan.

David was too young to worry much about what he wore, but he did worry about his hair.

> I hated having my hair cut. I had a bowl cut – as long as I could have it. Once, the hairdresser came to our house and cut my hair very short. I wouldn't go out of the house until I saw she had been round to my friend's house and cut his even shorter.

MAKE-UP

Sue's make-up was extravagant, too.

> I wore loads of mascara so my eyelashes looked like broomsticks. I wore thick eyeliner. I looked as though I had black eyes.

❗ Andrew remembers...

"The glam rock bands were wearing lots of very glittery clothes made of very shiny fabrics, with high heeled, ankle-length boots – stacks, as they were sometimes called. That's what you saw on TV but people didn't wear them really."

⬇ David Bowie brought a strange but glamorous style to the music stage in the early 1970s.

Music

Andrew, 1971

GLAM ROCK TO PUNK ROCK

Glam rock bands dominated the pop charts in the early 1970s. Then reggae bands (from Jamaica) and disco music got everyone dancing. Finally, punk rock bands upset the older generation with their angry political lyrics, studded jackets and spiky hair.

FIRST RECORD

Andrew can remember the first record he ever bought.

> *The first single I ever bought was 'Crazy Horses' by The Osmonds. I didn't realise there are some bands that girls liked and some bands that boys liked. So I was always a bit embarrassed about that – I'd bought a girl's record, for goodness sake!*

← American family pop group – The Osmonds. From left to right: Alan, Merill, Jay, Wayne, Donny and Jimmy.

! Sue remembers...

"I used to do all the disco dancing to 'Staying Alive' by the Bee Gees. We used to dance in a row – like line dancing – and all dance the same thing together. I went to a Bob Marley concert. I was a Michael Jackson fan when he was with the Jackson Five."

GLAM ROCK

Andrew was a big music fan all the way through the 1970s.

> *I got into glam rock when it was first happening. It just seemed so over the top. And of course my parents didn't like it and that made it all the more exciting.*

PUNK ROCK

When punk rock arrived on the scene in 1976, Andrew got into that too.

> Punk rock had a big influence on me. A lot of original punk bands, The Sex Pistols, Generation X and Siouxie and the Banshees, came from our area, Bromley. I loved the energy they put into their playing.

GUITAR HERO

Andrew took up the guitar and started to play in groups himself.

> I used to stand in front of the mirror and 'play' a tennis racket pretending to be a guitar hero, that I was in Slade. I do the same sort of pretending now.

Sometimes, Andrew's involvement with music clashed with his other interests.

> At the end of the 1970s the band I was playing in was asked to dress up like punks for an advert. I had to have pink hair. I couldn't get the dye out and I had to play in a chess tournament with pink hair.

Andrew still loves music and now plays in a glam rock tribute band.

↑ Sid Vicious, bass guitarist of one of the first punk bands – The Sex Pistols.

↓ Punk bands inspired a new look for young people.

23

Entertainment

TELEVISION, MOVIES AND HI-FIs

Even though colour televisions were replacing black-and-white television sets during the 1970s, the cinema remained popular. A new kind of movie hit the screens – the blockbuster. Blockbusters appealed to everyone and made more money than movies had ever made before. There were no CDs in the 1970s but records on vinyl and cassette tapes were played on new hi-fi (high fidelity) players.

DON'T GO IN THE WATER

The first blockbuster was *Jaws*, made in 1975, about a man-eating great white shark. *Jaws* had a menacing catchphrase – 'Don't go in the water!' David was only eight when he went to see *Jaws* and he took the catchphrase to heart.

> " *Whenever I heard the film's music I would say, 'He's coming! The shark's coming!' We lived near the beach and swam and played in the sea. I know there aren't great white sharks in the seas around Britain and I knew it then, but I'm still not very happy in the sea.* "

STAR WARS

In 1977, everyone was going to see the latest blockbuster, *Star Wars*. It made even more money than *Jaws*. For the first time film-makers made toys of the characters from the film, which proved massively popular with children. David remembers the toys.

↑ In 1977 *Star Wars* broke box office money-making records.

> " *Friends at school, especially the ones who were richer, collected* Star Wars *toys. We'd collected soccer stickers before, but not film merchandise.* "

GREASE

The music from the film *Grease* was as big a hit as the movie itself. Carole's daughter Lucy saw the film.

> ❝ *Everyone was crazy about* Grease *at school – Olivia Newton-John with her spray-on trousers. It was the first album where I thought, ooh! I want to be like everyone else.* ❞

⬇ John Travolta and Olivia Newton John (centre) in *Grease*.

Television

• •

The biggest revolution for television was the widespread change to colour. At the beginning of the 1970s Andrew's family had a black-and-white television.

> "*My brother and I kept trying to persuade Dad that it would be much better if we had a colour TV to watch educational programmes like* Life on Earth *or* The Ascent of Man. *Eventually we got a colour TV in the mid 1970s.*"

CASSETTE RECORDERS

Cassette recorders became more widely used in the 1970s, replacing less convenient, and more expensive reel-to-reel machines. Andrew got a portable cassette recorder for his 12th birthday.

> ❝ *It was the big thing! I always remember my father telling me – you don't just have to listen to pop music on that.* ❞

Strikes and discontent

Helen Passey's story

Helen, 1973

! Andrew remembers...

"*I loved it. We had to have all these candles and it was really very exciting. At the time, I think we were less dependent on electricity than we are today.*"

THREE-DAY WEEK

During the early 1970s Britain's economy – the management of its money – was in trouble. People could buy less for their money. To make things worse, coal miners refused to work overtime. Coal for power stations was in short supply and this led to power cuts. In January 1974, in the middle of a cold winter, the Prime Minister, Edward Heath, called for a three-day week to save electricity. Helen was 16 in 1974. She remembers the effect the power cuts had on everyday life.

" *My parents looked in the local paper to see the times when the electricity would be off in our area. People were worried about basic things like whether their frozen food would stay frozen. We wore extra layers to keep warm and were allowed to wear our coats in school. I did my homework by candlelight.* "

Businesses were affected as well.

" *I had a Saturday job selling electrical equipment. I was attempting to sell washing machines and kettles with no power to plug them into. We weren't selling anything at all.* "

← People used candlelight during power-cuts.

WINTER OF DISCONTENT

Helen remembers the winter of 1978-79, which has now become known as the 'Winter of Discontent'.

> " *I had just left university. It had been a very cold winter. All the public-sector unions had been on strike and no rubbish had been collected in London at all. Huge bin bags full of rubbish were piled up and Leicester Square was filled up with rubbish. It was really quite revolting.* "

⬆ Leicester Square in central London piled high with rubbish while refuse collectors went out on strike.

DRIVING TEST

Helen found that the strikes affected everything, even her driving test.

> " *I was trying to organise a driving test and I simply couldn't do it because the people who would book you in were on strike and refusing to take bookings.* "

IRISH TROUBLES

In Northern Ireland, trouble was growing between the Republicans, who wanted Northern Ireland to become united with the rest of Ireland, and the Loyalists, who wanted to remain part of the UK. The IRA – the Irish Republican Army – attacked British forces in Northern Ireland. Then in 1971, it threatened to bomb mainland Britain.

BOMBING CAMPAIGN

The first attack was on an army barracks in Aldershot in Hampshire. A car bomb exploded killing seven civilians. After that, the bombing campaign spread to the whole of the country and continued throughout the 1970s.

In 1973, Sue was working as a hairdresser in Selfridges, a department store in London, when an IRA bomb went off and destroyed the ground floor.

> " *I was working in the salon on the first floor. All of a sudden the whole building shook and glass broke and people were screaming and shouting. The ladies were running around with rollers in their hair. I was really, really scared. My parents were worried. There were no mobile phones to tell your family what had happened. It didn't really hit me until I got home and saw it on the TV and my mum burst out crying.* "

← A view through a shattered window opposite the Selfridges building, the day after the bomb. Amazingly only a few people were slightly injured.

Important changes

Decimalisation

In 1971, Britain copied other European countries to make its currency decimal. The old system of 12 pence to a shilling and 20 shillings to a pound became 100 new pence to a pound. It was much simpler, but people still grumbled about making the change.

European Economic Community

In January 1973 Britain, Ireland, Denmark and Norway joined France, Italy, West Germany, Belgium, Luxembourg and the Netherlands in the EEC – the European Economic Community. This meant that the population of the EEC was now bigger than that of the United States.

↑ It took a while for people to get used to the new system of currency.

FIRST WOMAN PRIME MINISTER

The voting age had been lowered from 21 to 18 in 1970. Helen had just missed being able to vote in 1974, but in 1979, at last, she had her first chance to vote. She felt that it was an important election.

The Conservatives won the general election and Margaret Thatcher became the first British woman prime minister. People looked forward to the 1980s with renewed hope that the economy's troubles were behind them.

> " The Labour Government had been in for five years. There had been non-stop strikes during the whole of that period. I think people had become fed up with a government that couldn't control the public-sector unions. "

← Margaret Thatcher waves to well-wishers outside 10 Downing Street, on her first day as prime minister.

Timeline

1970
1st January The British voting age is lowered from 21 to 18.
19th June Conservatives win election. Edward Heath becomes prime minister.

1971
9th February First British soldier killed in Northern Ireland.
15th February Decimal currency is introduced.

1972
22nd January Britain joins the European Economic Community.
30th January British troops kill 13 civilian demonstrators in Londonderry, Northern Ireland, in what became known as 'Bloody Sunday'.
21st September Asians with British passports are expelled from Uganda by dictator Idi Amin.

1973
3rd March One person killed and 250 injured in IRA bomb attacks on London.

1974
January Miners' overtime ban forces government to introduce a three-day week.
8th August President Nixon of America resigns after the Watergate scandal.
11th October Labour wins the general election with a majority of three seats. Harold Wilson becomes prime minister.
21st November 17 people are killed in Birmingham pubs by an IRA bomb.

1975
11th February Margaret Thatcher replaces Edward Heath as leader of the Conservative Party.
3rd October The Queen opens North Sea oil pipeline bringing oil to Britain.

1976
21st January The first passenger flights of two Concorde supersonic jet airliners, from London to Bahrain and from Paris to Rio de Janeiro.
August Water rationing is introduced during the driest summer of the century.

1977
7th June The Queen opens a week of festivities to celebrate her Silver Jubilee.

1978
26th July The first test-tube baby is born in Britain.

1979
January The streets are filled with rubbish during the 'Winter of Discontent'.
4th May Conservatives win the election. Margaret Thatcher becomes the first female British prime minister.

Glossary

Bowl cut A kind of hair cut that looks as though a bowl has been put on someone's head and the hair left showing has been cut off.

Calypso A Caribbean song with an off-beat (syncopated) rhythm.

Commissioner Someone who represents and works for an organisation or a country.

Community The people who live and work together in a neighbourhood.

Culture The art, music, ideas and beliefs of a particular society.

Curate An assistant clergyman in the Church of England.

Dictator A leader who rules a country with total authority.

Disciplinarian Someone who believes in enforcing strict rules.

Discontent A feeling of unhappiness or dissatisfaction.

Exotic A word that describes unfamiliar things from a foreign country.

Generation People within a certain age group. Teenagers are from a younger generation than their parents.

Immigrant Someone who leaves the country they were born in to make a new life in another country.

Inflation The way money loses its value and becomes worth less than before.

Merchandise Things for sale. Film merchandise is such things as toys and games based on the characters in a film.

Neighbourhood The area that surrounds the place where you live.

Overtime Extra time spent working outside regular work hours.

Package holiday A holiday arranged by a tour company that includes travel and somewhere to stay.

Public sector Services paid for by the tax payer such as hospitals, schools, fire stations and refuse collection.

Reel-to-reel A kind of tape recorder where the tape runs from one wheel, called a reel, to another.

Slide rule A calculator that looks like a ruler. Calculations are made by sliding two mathematic scales against each other.

Society A group of people that live and work together and share a way of life.

Strike When workers refuse to work because they are in dispute with their employers over pay or other issues.

Union An organisation that represents and stands up for the rights of groups of workers.